The Heart
of the
Matter

RANDALL THOMAS

ISBN 979-8-89428-138-4 (paperback)
ISBN 979-8-89428-139-1 (digital)

Christian Faith Publishing
832 Park Avenue
Meadville, PA 16335
www.christianfaithpublishing.com

Printed in the United States of America

An Introduction

I WANT TO emphasis the importance of looking at the context of the scripture you are reading.

Ask the questions the Holy Spirit brings to your attention while you are reading but sometimes just read and reread to acquaint yourself with verses you are reading. Remember that God gave us the questions what, where, when, how, who, and why. Asking the right question while reading will help us interpret what we are reading correctly.

Never be afraid to ask God for wisdom and always compare scripture with scripture. As Galatians warns about false teachers so Romans teaches us about sin and its effect on are lives, and about the importance of believing the Gospel of Jesus Christ. Romans also teaches us about the importance of reading our Bibles daily so we have the words of God guiding our actions.

So, I submit to you dear reader that, as in Romans, God tells us the path of salvation is always on the road of repentance and faith, so Ephesians is about God deciding how He would build His Temple. I simply conclude that God chose us (the believer) in Jesus because in Jesus is where all the believers blessings are found. Please remember Jesus's words.

You search the Scripture, for in them you think you have eternal life; and these are they which testify of Me. John 5:39

NOTES ON THE book of Galatians, Romans, and Ephesians.

I believe that the book of Romans is all about faith. Paul writes about how faith is a gift and how it can be exercised. Faith is important because it is the only way to please God (Hebrews 11:6). In Romans, Paul gives a special greeting to those who believe the gospel of Jesus Christ. He also writes about how for a long time he had wanted to come and see them. Paul tells them about how he longed to be there so he could preach the good news to them (Romans 1:16–17). Then Paul writes about the condition of man and how God deals with the hearts of all mankind.

So Paul uses the word *truth* so we understand. The word is used in Romans 1:19, 2:2, 2:8, and 2:20.

So in chapter 1:18 and following, the truth that men try to suppress is that God is real, and He has made it known to all mankind (v. 19). Some acknowledge Him as God and some don't. Some are thankful and some turn from this truth, and because of their turning away from what God has shown them, God takes action. God does not condemn them, but they condemn themselves because they go after their own desires. So God gave them over to do what they wanted. Chapter 1:20 explains His eternal power and Godhead. In Acts 14:1–22, we read Paul was telling the people of Lystra and Derbe about Jesus, and Paul healed a man. Then they said the gods have come down to us in the likeness of men. Then Paul and Barnabas said they were men just as them. Paul told them to turn from these vanities unto the living God, who made heaven and earth, and all things therein. So Paul proclaimed God's power, then Paul proclaimed another attribute of God, that He did good and gave us rain from heaven and fruitful seasons, filling our hearts with food and gladness. So in these verses, we see the Godhead displays His power, His long-suffering, and His love for His creation. I believe when the word *Godhead* is used in the scriptures, it is a term about the fullness containing all of His attributes, mainly God's deity. So this truth is that God is real, and He is powerful and holy.

I believe that these verses in chapter 1:19–20 explain that in a person's lifetime, they will have a moment when they will either side with God and acknowledge Him or they won't.

In Romans 2:2, we find the next truth, that God's judgment is based on the truth. In chapter 1, we have seen the moral decline of those who turn away from believing that God is real. These people have been given over to the lusts of their own hearts, so we see from this statement that this decline is about our morality. Even creation speaks out in judgment in these matters; these lusts go against the natural order of creation itself (chapter 1:26–27). So we see in chapter 2 that God's judgment plays no favorites (v. 11); there is no respect for persons with God.

Paul also writes that these evil actions will suffer consequences (v. 6): "Who will render to every man according to his deeds." In chapter 2, mankind is given the responsibility to choose right over wrong and what the reward is, tribulation and anguish upon every soul of man that does evil, but glory, honor, and peace, to every man that worketh good. In Matthew 7:7–11, Jesus Himself says we have the ability to know the difference between good and bad. So the next time Paul uses the word *truth* in chapter 2:8, he is writing about God's redemption power. Like others, I believe this bears out in the context; Paul is writing about matters of the heart. As in verse 5, some seek for good, and others seek only for their self-interests. The final question is what have you done with Jesus, have you believed His gospel, or have you turned your back on it (v. 16)?

The next time Paul uses the word *truth* here in chapter 2 is found in verse 20, the truth in the law, and Paul goes on to write about the abuses people commit by doing those things they know are wrong. I simply believe that chapter 2 is about God's judgment and its consequences rather than how we are justified.

So let's agree that Paul is writing about how we do things that bring about God's indignation and that we are all guilty. Then in chapter 2:15, Paul writes about the work of the law that is written on our hearts. He goes on to talk about us as having certain rules we accept of behavior or we don't. So we have a sense of morality within us whether we believe in God or not. An example of this kind of behavior is found in John 8:1–11. In the context of this event, Jesus told them, "He who is without sin among you, let him throw a stone at her first," but nobody did.

Their guilty conscience made them leave because they knew they had committed something wrong too, and Jesus did what He was sent to do, He forgave her (John 3:17).

Let me say some things about what we have read so far. We have seen that God's indignation is directed to those who turn away from the truth and receive the consequences of their decisions.

Paul writes a lot about good versus bad, and it almost seems like we get to heaven by our own behavior, but if we believe that, we have come to the wrong conclusion, and here is why.

Romans 3:19–20: "By the deeds of the law no flesh will be justified in God's sight, for by the law is the knowledge of sin." See also Romans 7:7–12. So the law reveals the sin in our lives, and as Paul has proven, we are all guilty. Paul has also written in Romans 2:13 that not the hearers of the law are just in God's sight, but the doers of the law will be justified. So what does the law compel us to do? The answer is found in Luke 10:25–37. The lawyer asked Jesus what he had to do to inherit eternal life, and Jesus asked the lawyer, "What is written in the law? What is your reading of it?"

The lawyer answered and used Scripture and said, "You shall love the Lord your God with all your heart, and with all your soul, and with all your strength, and with all your mind, and your neighbor as yourself."

Jesus answered and said, "You have answered rightly; do this and you will live." I believe that the law compels us to do exactly what the lawyer quoted to Jesus, to trust in God. In Galatians 3:24, the law was our schoolmaster to bring us unto Christ. So let us think about the downward spiral of our morals when we don't acknowledge

God; our conscience first becomes compromised in chapter 1:24, then in verse 26, our conscience becomes complaisant, then in verse 28, the conscience becomes corrupt.

We find ourselves in an awful place where we are missing all the blessings that God had planned for us. We have also seen how we have a responsibility to choose right rather than wrong.

So whether we are Jews or Gentiles, we are all guilty. So far, there have been a lot of negative things written, but when we get to Romans 3:21, we find the word *but*, we find the good news, for now, there is hope. "But now the righteousness of God apart from the law is revealed, being witnessed by the Law and the Prophets, even the righteousness of God, through faith in Jesus Christ, to all and on all who believe."

So in Romans 3:21–26, Paul is saying again that we all are guilty, but God is displaying His righteousness by sending His only begotten Son to pay the penalty of our sin for us; thus, we can have forgiveness by placing our faith in Jesus Christ. This way, God has displayed His loving kindness for us and He can be just and justified in forgiving us.

So Paul goes on in verses 27–31 and asks the question, since faith is the way we who believe that Jesus paid the penalty in full for our redemption, where is boasting? The simple answer is, we cannot boast because it is all about God's mercy and grace. So Paul also says that any person, whether they have lived under the law of commandments as Jews, or if they as a Gentile without the knowledge of the Jewish law, can still be redeemed because there is only one God who can and will save us if we believe the Gospel. So Paul asks the question, do we make void the Law? He says no, but rather we establish the Law. Remember what the lawyer said about the law, how it was supposed to compel him to trust in God and love Him. Jesus gave the Holy Spirit to us who believe to convict us of our sin (John 16:5–11) just as the law reveals our sin and compels us to love God and go to Him for forgiveness. So I submit to you, dear reader, that the Law and the work of the Holy Spirit have the same purpose: to have faith in God and to love Him with all our hearts. Thus, we establish the law.

Paul goes on in chapter 4 to write about Abraham's faith, and since he believed God's promise that he would have a son, born of his own body even though he and Sarah were both beyond the normal years of childbearing, God imputed righteousness to Abraham. Paul goes on to say in verse 23, it was not written for his sake alone that it was imputed to him, but also for us. It shall be imputed to us who believe in Him who raised up Jesus our Lord from the dead, who was delivered up because of our offenses, and was raised because of our justification.

So I conclude that the Law reveals the sins we have committed and puts us under condemnation, but when we believe the gospel and put our faith in Jesus, we are justified before God. So then Paul writes in Romans 5, Therefore, having been justified by faith, we have peace with God through our Lord Jesus Christ." Remember the first three fruits of the Holy Spirit: love, joy, and peace (Galatians 5:22). Paul writes about how we have access all because of what Jesus did, which gives us hope, and the assurance of our salvation is sure no matter the circumstances we find ourselves in, all because of the love of God has been poured out in our hearts by the Holy Spirit who was given to us. Paul keeps on writing about even though we were still sinners, Christ died for us. Paul keeps on and adds more of the blessings we receive when we trust in what Jesus did for us—we will even escape the wrath of God through Him, but the apostle Paul has more blessings to tell us about the atoning work that Jesus did for us when He went to the cross in our place. Jesus made it possible for us to be reconciled with God. We are no longer enemies of God but placed in God's favor. Oh, how thankful we should be. Praise His holy name.

My thinking on reading the first three chapters of Romans is that I see that I have the ability to choose right over wrong, and sometimes I choose the wrong over the right for whatever reason. This convinces me that I have a sinful nature. Paul goes on to write about where this sinful nature came from in Romans 5:12: "Therefore, just as through one man sin entered the world, and death through sin, and thus death spread to all men, because all sinned." David wrote about it in Psalm 51:4. So when Adam disobeyed God's command, he passed on to us his own sinful nature. Then Paul writes about how that by one man's righteous act and His total obedience, many will be made righteous. To be clear, that man's name was, and is, Jesus Christ.

The next chapter in Romans starts us off on our journey as believers. Chapters 6–7 deals with our relationship with our Savior. So we have been justified because Jesus paid the penalty in our place, and we stand in God's favor by His grace and mercy. So Paul asks, "Shall we continue in sin, that grace may abound?" God forbid is the answer! Paul goes on to say how can we live in constant sin when we, through the power of the Holy Spirit, have been made free from the power of sin by Jesus's death and resurrection. We are also admonished to realize that our old sinful nature has been crucified with Christ, and we are to realize that our old sinful nature has been buried just as Jesus was buried, and we also should count ourselves alive from the dead and walk in newness of life just as Jesus rose from the grave to the glory of God the Father. Paul says it this way: "Therefore do not let sin reign in your mortal body, that you should obey it in its lusts. And do not present your members as instruments of unrighteousness to sin, but present yourselves to God as being alive from the dead, and your members as instruments of righteousness to God" (Romans 6:12–13).

You might ask how do I do this? Maybe this answer is too simple but it is all-powerful: by faith. Galatians 2:20: "I have been crucified with Christ; it is no longer I who live, but Christ lives in me; and the life which I now live in the flesh I live by faith in the Son of God, who loved me and gave Himself for me."

Remember what David said in Psalms 119:11: "Thy word have I hid in mine heart, that I might not sin against thee." Also in Habakkuk 2:4: "…the just shall live by faith."

If I judge myself, I see a man who has made many mistakes but God in His mercy has forgiven me, and still, in my humanness, I will still make more mistakes, but I have faith in God who will guide me by the Holy Spirit who lives in me. When we get drawn into the lusts of our hearts and we want to do whatever it is, we have a helper (the Holy Spirit) who is able to change the circumstances of our situation and keep us from doing what we want. I know that sin is still alive in my members. Sin was not crucified; I was, so I—being in union with Christ in His death, burial, and resurrection, and because of the presence and power of the Holy Spirit—have the ability to say no to those lusts that would compel me to sin against God. Again, remember Romans 6:12–13 and also 1 Corinthians 10:13: "No temptation has overtaken you except such as is common to man; but God is faithful, who will not allow you to be tempted beyond what you are able, but with the temptation will also make the way of escape, that you may be able to bear it." Have you seen the Holy Spirit work in your lives this way? I have given the glory to Him who loves us.

Let us take some time to see what we have learned so far:

1. We learned that mankind has a moral calamity: we either acknowledge God as our creator or we choose not to.
2. We learned that if we choose not to, we are given over to our own evil desires.
3. We learned that if we think that we have the high moral ground and we judge others, we condemn ourselves also because we are all guilty of doing something wrong.
4. We learned that if we obey the truth, we can and will get the reward of eternal life just as those who choose not to obey the truth will get theirs.
5. We learned that God's Law is the standard by which we will be judged and that no flesh (or human being) will be justified by keeping the Law's requirements because by the Law, we acquired the knowledge of sin (or wrongdoing) in our lives.
6. We learned that the hearing of the Law does not justify us but that the doers of the Law will be justified.
7. We are introduced to Abraham who was a doer of the Law (even though the Law had not been given yet) because he believed God's promise and that righteousness was imputed to him because of his faith that he believed God could and is able to do what He promises.
8. We also learned that righteousness would be imputed to us. Also if we believe the Gospel in this, we learn that righteousness came by faith and not by works.

9. We also understand that the Law showed us our sinful nature and the Law also compels us to be a doer of the Law by exercising the gift of faith by which we need to love and trust Him.

10. We also found out where this sinful nature came from (in Adam) and who came into this world to defeat it (Jesus Christ).

11. We also have come to understand that we, the believers, have been justified by faith in Jesus Christ because He paid the penalty for our sins when He went to the cross in our place, and now we are placed in God our Father's favor because Jesus's righteousness has been given to us.

12. We have come to understand that since we have been justified by faith, we have also been reconciled to God. This statement is not only factual but is a matter of worship. Romans 5:11: "We also rejoice in God through our Lord Jesus Christ, through whom we have now received the reconciliation."

Next, in Romans 6–7, Paul asks some questions about how we are to proceed in our walk (our daily lives) with our Lord and Savior. Romans 6:1: "Shall we continue in sin that God's grace may abound?" The answer is in very strong language in Greek: "God forbid." Paul says that we have been placed into union with Christ through the word picture of baptism. So we were baptized into His death, and we were raised up to walk in newness of life. So we are to, by faith, realize we are dead and that Jesus is alive in us, and through the power of God the Holy Spirit, we are to present our bodies to God for His service. Thus, we will be servants unto righteousness. Let us look at how Paul, through the guidance of the Holy Spirit, writes this: "Likewise, you also, reckon yourselves to be dead indeed to sin, but alive to God in Christ Jesus our Lord. Therefore, do not let sin reign in your mortal body, that you should obey it in its lusts. And do not present your members as instruments of unrighteousness to sin, but present yourselves to God as being alive from the dead, and your members as instruments of righteousness to God. For sin shall not have dominion over you, for you are not under law but under grace" (Romans 6:11–14). So here in these verses, we have responsibility and blessings. I have a question: do we see that it is not us who is doing the work but that it is the Holy Spirit working through us and for us? I say this because we are to reckon ourselves dead and to yield ourselves to God.

The question in verse 6:1 is answered by showing us that by faith we have been united with Jesus, and the next question in verse 6:15 has to do with our commitment to Jesus. Shall we commit sins because we are not under the Law but under grace? "God forbid" is the same answer. Paul goes on to say if we yield ourselves to one master, we can't be the servants of another. Jesus Himself said we cannot be the servants of two masters (Matthew 6:24). So Paul's question is a contrast between the Law (which reveals sin and condemns it) and grace, which is God's favor and empowers the believer.

Paul has another question in Romans 7:7, but before he gets to the question, he writes about the law of marriage. The woman is bound by this law to her husband as long as he lives, but if the husband dies, she is free to remarry (v 7:4–6). Paul explains, "My brethren, you also have become dead to the Law through the body of Christ, that you may be married to another, to Him who was raised from the dead, that we should bear fruit to God. For when we were in the flesh, the sinful passions which were aroused by the Law were at work in our members to bear fruit to death. But now we have been delivered from the Law, having died to what we were held by, so that we should serve in the newness of the Spirit and not in the oldness of the letter."

I think the point is this: Our union with Christ, not to the Law, allows us the liberty to serve God in the power of the Holy Spirit because the Law brings about death, but the Holy Spirit brings life. We also see that the husband is the one who died, not the Law. So if we abide by the Law, our sinful passions are aroused by the Law, and that brings death because the Law reveals sin but cannot give life. But if we abide in the Holy Spirit, we can bring forth fruit unto God.

So then the question of verse 7: is the Law sin? "God forbid" again is the answer. Paul goes on to say he would not have known what sin is unless the Law had revealed it. So since the command-ment came, sin revived, and by what is just and Holy, sin killed me. So Paul has another question in verse 13: "Has then what is good become death to me?" "God forbid!" again is the answer. But sin, that it might appear sin, was producing death in me through what is good so that sin through the commandment might become exceed-ingly sinful. Here is the New Living Translation way of translating (7:13): "But how can that be? Did the Law, which is good, cause my death? Of course not! Sin used what was good to bring about my condemnation to death. So we can see how terrible sin really is. It (sin) uses God's commands for its own evil purposes."

Romans 7:14: "For we know that the Law is spiritual; (because it came from God) but I am carnal, (I am a human being or of the flesh) sold under sin." I inherited a sinful nature because my forefa-thers were all sinners too. But now being united with Jesus, I have a new nature, but sometimes I don't follow my new nature's directions. Why does that happen?

In verses 15–23, Paul talks about this problem. There are three laws that are mentioned here in these verses: the Law of God the law (or principle), "that when I do something good, that evil is present with me" (v. 21); and the law of my mind, which delights in the Law and in following and seeing the Holy Spirit work in and through and for me (v. 22); and "but I also see another law working against me that is in my members," the law of sin (v. 23).

Have you seen the Holy Spirit work in your life when you wanted to do something that your mind told you that you knew God was against, but the Holy Spirit changed the circumstances of your situation so you couldn't? This kind of situation proves to me that when I want to do something I know is wrong and I try to avoid doing it even though I still want to, that the Holy Spirit is there to help me in my temptation. This kind of situation proves that my flesh is weak and that sin is still alive in my members. Paul argues from another point of the question: why do I do those things that I hate? The answer is still the same: sin is still alive in my members, and my flesh is weak. So I am living in a body that has sin in its members, my eyes, my tongue, my ears; there are more members than just these three. They can be used for good purposes, but sometimes they are not. I wanted to do something I knew was good, but I didn't; in fact, I missed the opportunity because the sin in my members was keeping me from understanding what the good thing to do was. Maybe that was part of the problem Peter faced in Galatians 2:11–14. I don't really know. What I do know is sin is still alive in my members, and sin causes all these problems. Thank God He gave us the Holy Spirit to help us.

Thank God again for 1 John 1:9 and 10. Let me say again that sin was not crucified, but my old nature was. In Matthew 5:27–30, Jesus was teaching about how adultery was forbidden by those who taught the scriptures in Old Testament times. Then Jesus went on to say that adultery was a matter of the heart, so the sin of adultery is not just about the physical act but also about our innermost spiritual desires to be right with God. So then He says if your eye causes you to lust after her, pluck it out. Jesus is speaking hyperbolically (the use of extremes, which were not to be taken literally; the writer of Proverbs 23:1–3 used the same method). So Jesus was talking about the members of our body and how sin uses them to bring about our condemnation.

As a mere human, I don't have control over what might come into my view, say as I am driving my car, but I do have control over what I stare at. So let us go back to Romans 7; as we read chapter 7, these things come to mind. Paul's emotions were involved: love and hate; his mind, what was good or bad; his will, what he wanted and what he did not want to do. What can we learn? Do we see the conflict in our being human beings? When I was alive before I met Jesus, there was no conflict; I just did whatever I pleased that made me happy. I was alive in my person, but I was dead unto God. But after I believed in Jesus, I was born again, and I found myself alive to God but dead because of sin in my members.

So when I trusted in Christ, I found myself in conflict within myself because sin was still alive in my members. So now after accepting Jesus as my savior, I have a new life that is filled with conflict because I want to please Him, but sin is still alive in my members. As long as I am in this body, this conflict will still go on.

So what is this conflict all about? Galatians 5:17: "For the flesh lusts against the Holy Spirit, and the Holy Spirit against the flesh; and these are contrary to one another, so that you do not do the things that you wish." So we as Christians are in a war zone because sin is still alive, and it uses my members as instruments of unrighteousness. Remember our old man was crucified with Christ, and our new man was brought to life through and by and being found in Him, and at that moment, He gave us the Holy Spirit to help us. Can we have victory while we are still in this body? Galatians 5:16: "I say then: Walk in the Holy Spirit, and you shall not fulfill the lust of the flesh." Are we always walking under the guidance of God's Word and the Holy Spirit? For myself, I can say no I haven't, but I also know that Jesus said that He would never leave me nor forsake me (Hebrews 13:5).

Can I say that I will not make mistakes while I am studying God's Word and following the Holy Spirit? I am sure I will find myself doing or saying something I wish I hadn't. Again, we can go back to what Paul wrote in Romans 7:21–23: "I find then a law (a principle) that evil is present with me, the one who wills to do good. For I delight in the Law of God according to the inward man. But I see another law in my members, warring against the law of my mind, and bringing me into captivity to the law of sin which is in my members."

Let me say something here: the conflict I see in my life proves to me that I am a born-again believer. The conflict is not about two natures at war against each other but rather a war between two realms of spiritual realities, the lust of the flesh (our unredeemed humanness) and the Holy Spirit, who was given to us when we trusted in Jesus. The things that I do that I hate, I take full responsibility for, but when I see a victory in my life, I give thanks to God because He was and is the one who accomplished it. So my responsibility is to do what Galatians 5:24 says, "And they that are Christ's have crucified the flesh with the affections and lusts." So we do not have to live in despair, but we can live in joy and peace as we abide in Christ and give the fruit of the Spirit back to God in our exercise of being faithful, humble, and displaying self-control toward Him. In John 15:4,

Jesus said, "Abide in Me." In Romans 7:24, Paul asks the question, "O wretched man that I am! Who shall deliver me from the body of this death?" Verse 25 has the victory song of thanksgiving: "I thank God through Jesus Christ our Lord." I think Paul has in mind here in these verses what he writes about in 1 Corinthians 15 and also 2 Corinthians 5, where he writes about our new bodies. First John 3:2 and also 1 Peter 1:4 also speak of these same things. The last part of verse 25, I want to put in my own words: So then, with the mind (that inner part of me who I really am since I met Jesus and submits to the Word of God as to my behavior) recognizes the fact that I am still in this body (flesh) where there is a moral sense of right and wrong, and sin can be seen by my actions when I do the things that I deep down in my inner man hate.

This is not about mind over matter but rather a matter of whom we submit our will to. Since I met Jesus, I know that I still have sin in me while I am still in this mortal body, but thanks be to Jesus, I don't have sin on me. Do we submit to the leading of the Holy Spirit or to the fleshly desires of our own humanness? So then in Romans 8:1–2, we have the words of praise and thanksgiving: "There is therefore now no condemnation to them which are in Christ Jesus, who walk not after the flesh but after the Holy Spirit. For the law of the Holy Spirit of life in Christ Jesus has made me free from the law of sin and death. O praise His Holy name and Amen."

So in chapter 8:3, we have the reason for not being condemned: Jesus came to deliver us. Paul goes on to write about the contrast between walking in the Holy Spirit and walking under the influence of the flesh. Being under the guidance and submitting ourselves to the Holy Spirit (whose job it is to guide us into the truth), we will find real life and peace, but those who live according to the flesh (as according to 1 John, the things of this world) will only find unrest. For to be carnally minded is death, but to be spiritually minded is life and peace.

As we read here in Romans chapters 7–8, do we get a sense of God's Word showing us how important it is with all of our hearts to love, trust, and obey Him? Let me jump ahead to chapter 8:12, which says, in my own words, are we not debtors to live according to the Holy Spirit rather than the lusts of our own flesh because Jesus paid the penalty on our behalf?

So back to the verses we were just looking at. Since we are living our lives according to the principles that God's Holy Word has given us, don't we feel a sense of responsibility and loyalty to follow the Holy Spirit's leading? Don't we get a sense of the Holy Spirit's presence in our lives when we struggle with the circumstances in our lives? So then can we see that the Holy Spirit bears witness to our spirit and confirms to us as a matter of fact, not just feeling, that we are children of God, and praise God we are not just children but heirs with Jesus. We also have a marvelous future.

Paul writes here in verse 18: "For I consider that the sufferings of this present time are not worthy to be compared with the glory which shall be revealed in us." The apostle says that the creation is going through birth pains, waiting for the glorious liberty that is awaiting our total redemption from all these birth pains we are going through as we experience the change in our lives as we come to maturity in Christ. Paul writes about our adoption (the redemption of our body) and how that is the hope that we have being found in Christ. Paul writes about how not only Jesus is making intercession for us but that the Holy Spirit is also doing the same. We have seen that Paul had the conflict in himself that he wrote about in Romans 7, and we know that this same conflict abides in us also. What does this conflict mean to you and me? What is its purpose?

Romans 8:28–29: "And we know that all things work together for good to those who love God, to those who are the called according to His purpose. For whom He foreknew (the ones who believed the gospel), He also predestined to be conformed to the image of His Son." Do we see the purpose of this conflict? I believe it's all about having us in a place where we are totally committed to following in Jesus's footsteps, whatever the circumstances—whether we think the circumstances are bad or good, we will still trust our Heavenly Father. So I know that when I want to do good, evil is still present with me, but I also know that the Holy Spirit is with me and that He will help me. So in this life, I want to be more like my wonderful Lord and Savior, but I see in myself that I still come up short. I judge myself that way. But I see hope in verse 31: "What then shall we say to these things? If God is for us, who can be against us?" Do you see the reassurance and joy in this question? God Himself gave us His Son to save us and bring us into His kingdom.

Then in verse 37: "Yet in all these things we are more than conquerors through Him who loved us." Paul goes on to say that nothing in creation can separate us from the love of God, which is in Christ Jesus our Lord. Let us stop a minute and think about the verses in chapters 7 and 8. We have been learning about our human condition that Jesus has delivered us from the penalty of sin, but we also know that sin is still alive in my members. We have also seen that God decided to conform the ones who believed the gospel into the image of His Son. I simply believe, since these verses were written in the past tense (v. 29–30), that God made these decisions before He started His work of creation, simply before He said, "Let there be light." Do you believe that God is using the struggles of the life we are in now to love and trust God with all of our hearts? Could we say without the conflict, we would not know the victory we have in abiding in Jesus?

As we think on these things, let me go on to Romans 9:22–24: "What if God, wanting to show His wrath and to make His power known, endured with much long-suffering the vessels of wrath prepared for destruction (it does not say here that God prepared these vessels for wrath, but it does say they were prepared. Romans 1 says that when mankind turns from acknowledging our Creator as God and being thankful, God gives us up to the lusts of our own flesh, so I submit to you, dear reader, that these vessels were preparing themselves for destruction), and that He might make known the riches of His glory on the vessels of mercy, which He had prepared beforehand for glory, even us whom He called, not of the Jews only, but also of the Gentiles?"

Let me go on to say this: Just as these vessels were preparing themselves for destruction, God in His mercy decided in the past how He would prepare these vessels of mercy for glory. Thus, we have been learning about the purpose of the conflict, to love God and trust Him with all of our hearts. So do we submit and humble ourselves before our Lord and trust our instruction manual, the Bible, on how to live our lives? We have a choice: we can either stumble into sin because of our own lusts, or we can submit to the leading of the Holy Spirit (He will always show us the truth if we just listen) through reading God's Word and asking Jesus to give us wisdom.

Let me say this: does not this conflict confirm that the Holy Spirit is in me and helping me to overcome my weaknesses and be more like my Lord and Savior? I submit to you, dear reader, the Christian life is a growing experience. Second Peter 1:5 says to add to your faith certain things. In 1 John 4, John writes not to simply believe everything you hear but to test it against what God's Word has to say about the matter. Paul tells Timothy in 2 Timothy to be strong in the grace of Jesus and to study so he (Timothy) can refute any false teachers that come into the church. In 1 John 2:12–14, John writes about three levels of maturity that we have in Christ: little children, those who believed the Gospel; young men, those who have believed the Gospel and have come to know sound doctrine; and to fathers, as to those who know God in all His fullness and see God working out in them all things for His glory and their good. There are more verses of Scripture, I am sure, that give us the truth about how we are born into our Lord's household and how we grow up. These things we are writing about are why I interpret Romans 9: the last part of 23, that God decided in the past how He would bring us into glory. Remember, this book is about faith, and matured faith has this already accomplished because God has already decided.

Let us go on to Romans chapters 9–11. Many commentaries regard these chapters as pertaining to Israel only, with the focus on Israel as a nation and not on individuals. I see that the subject is not just about Israel as a nation but about who the true people of Israel are, or in other words, who the true children of God are. The people of Israel came through Abraham and his seed (Isaac), but the real people of God came through the child of promise, Jesus. Let me say this: Isaac was born because of Abraham's faith and by the power of God, who can make things happen that seem impossible. Go back and read Genesis 18:1–15. So the real people of God are not just children of the flesh but rather children of the promise, or in other words, they are the true children because of their faith.

Paul goes on and writes about how God chose Jacob over Esau, even though Esau was the firstborn. Notice also that God made His choice before the boys were born. So what do we understand here? God is sovereign and omniscient; He has the final authority and the knowledge to do what He pleases. Paul goes on and tells us why He, God, loved Jacob, but He hated Esau. Proverbs 6:16–19 tells us what God hates, but this hate here is more than just about our behavior because the children were not yet born. This kind of hate that God has for certain people I cannot explain, but I will say this: have you had someone who said they loved you and proved it to you, turn around and say they hated you, even though you knew inside of yourself that they really loved you? I don't know what else to write about this kind of hate. I do know this, that God's thoughts are higher than my thoughts and His ways are higher than mine. Isaiah 55:6–9.

Let us go back to 9:11. The purpose of God according to election (the way God chooses) might stand, not of works but of Him who calls, or in other words, God wants us to respond to Him. The Pharaoh wouldn't, so the Pharaoh's heart was hardened. Jacob responded he wanted the birthright, which Esau gave to Jacob for a meal. Jacob was minded toward the things that had a spiritual side of the family's unity, but Esau did not care about that. Thus, the Jewish nation was propagated through the loins of Jacob instead of Esau. Paul goes on and writes about God's right to choose whom He pleases because He is the Creator of all things. God has called out to His people, but Israel, for the most part, did not respond (Romans 10:21).

Since Israel, for the most part, did not respond to the Gospel, the Gentiles were offered the same message the Jews rejected, even though the Gentiles were not His people as a chosen nation. Also, in Romans 10, Paul explains how God chooses those who will be saved in verses 9–13. So let me say this: the salvation offered to the Jews as a nation in Deuteronomy 30:11–20 is the same message as the gospel of Christ, that we are to trust in God with all our heart. Let me go on and say our faith is a gift from God, but we also must respond to the message by admitting we are sinners and ask for forgiveness (1 John 1:9). One more thing to remember is that our salvation is not based on our merit but solely on God's mercy. Paul gives a summary of what he writes about in Romans 9:30–33. Paul also gives us a summary of what he writes about in chapter 10:16–21.

After reading chapter 10, we understand that our salvation is not based on works but on our hearts, and that's why Jacob was chosen over Esau. According to Hebrews 12:14–17, Esau wanted the blessing, but he found no reason to repent. Esau did things that he knew grieved his mom and dad, but he did them anyway (Genesis 26:34). On the other hand, Jacob obeyed his mom, and he received the blessing, even though he received it by deceit. Jacob and Esau were both sinners, just like all of us, but if you read about Jacob's life in Genesis 27–33, you will see the difference between Jacob's heart and Esau's. Read Genesis 32:9–10.

Let me say this: God knows all of our hearts because He is omniscient. He knew Jeremiah's heart before Jeremiah was born, chapter 1, verses 4–8. God knew David's heart also, 1 Samuel 13:14 and Acts 13:22. God also knew Paul's heart, Galatians 1:15 and Romans 1:1–6. So let me say this again: God knows every person's heart. Romans 10:9, "That if you confess with your mouth the Lord Jesus and believe in your heart that God has raised Him from the dead, you will be saved." Verse 10 says, "For with the heart one believes unto righteousness, and with the mouth, confession is made unto salvation." Paul goes on to write about how we can hear this message of hope (by God sending preachers to proclaim the message), which is God's Word. So the message is the gospel of Christ, and we believe it through faith. How does faith come? Paul answers the question in Romans 10:17: "So faith comes by hearing God's Word." So then you have to hear it to believe it, and you have to confess that you're a sinner to receive it. What we have been thinking about here in these verses, James says this in chapter 1:18: "Of His (God's) own will, He brought us forth by the word of truth, that we might be a kind of first fruits of His creatures."

You might wonder why all this importance is placed on the condition of our heart. Isaiah 66:1–2: "Thus says the Lord: 'Heaven is My throne, and earth is My footstool. Where is the house that you will build Me? And where is the place of My rest? For all those things My hand made, and all those things exist,' says the Lord, 'but on this one will I look: On him who is poor and of a contrite spirit, and who trembles at My word.'"

Isaiah 57:15: "For thus says the High and Lofty One, Who inhabits eternity, whose name is Holy: I dwell in the high and holy place, with him who has a contrite and humble spirit."

Psalm 34:18: "The Lord is near to those who have a broken heart and saves such as have a contrite spirit."

Did you notice in Genesis 32:9–10 that Jacob did not feel worthy of all the truth that God had given him? Jacob felt remorse, and at the same time, he was thankful. I believe in those verses, we get a view of Jacob's heart. Let me stop here a minute.

I want to go back to Isaiah 66:1–2 and think about what is written. Do we get a sense of what God says here, that God had already made these decisions sometime in the past? I do.

So just as Jacob was chosen because Jacob had a heart that was concerned about the birthright, which had a covenant promise from God with it, we also were chosen because we believed the gospel of Christ through the work of the Holy Spirit. Jacob's journey to find a wife led him into a personal contact with our Lord, just as our experience with the Holy Spirit brought us to the place of repentance and faith. God, who at various times and in various ways spoke in times past to the fathers by the prophets, has in these last days spoken to us by His Son (Hebrews 1:1).

So what have we learned? Faith is a gift; we have a responsibility to respond by exercising it. Our salvation is not based on our behavior but on our hearts. God is the only one who can know our hearts (Jeremiah 17:7–10; 2 Timothy 2:19). Abiding in Jesus and His Word abiding in us is the only way we can overcome the power of sin. We are to live our lives not by our own determinate will but by submitting our will to God's. The law was not given to justify us but rather to reveal our sins and to bring us to Christ. God has the right to choose whoever He pleases because He alone knows the hearts of all mankind. We also see that the purpose of God according to election is to respond to His call to love and trust Him no matter the circumstances, and, since God is sovereign (the potter over the clay, as with Pharaoh, who had evil intentions), to use whatever vessel for His purpose to show His power and to proclaim His name over all the earth. Rahab got the message and saved her family (Joshua 2:1–21). God is the only one who can build His place of rest because He alone knows the hearts of all mankind.

Since we have been writing about how God chooses, I want to write about when God decided to build His temple. I submit to you, dear reader, that God decided to build His temple before He started His work of creation, or in other words, before He said, "Let there be light." There are several verses we need to look at; they either say "from the beginning," "before time began," "before the foundation of the earth was formed," or the verse was written in the past tense. All these verses have to do with God's decisions about building His temple:

1. 1 Peter 1:20: Jesus was foreordained before the foundation of the world to come and pay the price for our sins.
2. Titus 1:1–3: God promised to give eternal life to those who would believe the gospel of Christ and that preaching would be the way He would send the message before time began.
3. 2 Thessalonians 2:13–14: From the beginning, God chose the Holy Spirit to be the one who would bring us to the place of repentance and faith.
4. 1 Timothy 1:9: God would give us the grace we need to do what He gives us to do before time began.
5. Romans 8:28–30: In eternity past, God decided that we, the believers, would be conformed to the image of His Son, be justified, and be glorified; all these things were predetermined.
6. Ephesians 2:10: God had a plan and purpose for our lives before time began.
7. Ephesians 1:4: Just as He chose us in Him (Jesus) before the foundation of the world.

Let us not be confused here on point 7. God chose us in Christ when we believed in the gospel of Christ, and at that moment in time, the Holy Spirit was given to us. We were not predestined to be believers, but since God knows the hearts of all mankind, He knew we would believe. We were not chosen to abide by God's Law because it brings about wrath; as humans, we are all sinners. So God chose us in Christ because in Him is the place of our redemption. Look at the context of Ephesians (this is *very* important): Paul is writing to believers, the saints, and the faithful in Christ Jesus.

Since I believe that God decided to build His house before He said, "Let there be light," I believe Ephesians is telling us *why* we were chosen in Christ. Let me say this again: God chose us when we believed the Gospel of Christ, and we received the Holy Spirit at that moment in time, and we were born again and became children of God. As we think about God building His house, where would He build it, or better yet, in whom would He build it? The answer: He chose us in Him (Ephesians 1:4). Again, He decided how to build His house before He said, "Let there be light."

This house is made up of repentant sinners who found forgiveness because they believe that Jesus paid their sin debt. So who were we forgiven by, and where do all our blessings come from? Of course, the answer is in Jesus. Let me say this: this building is not being built out of the work of His hands, like Adam and Eve were, but rather out of His faithfulness, long-suffering, grace, and mercy.

Let us think about this little word *in*. Dr. D. Edmond Hiebert writes, "This living union between Christ and the believer is made prominent by the repeated use of the little word *in* which occurs no less than one hundred and twenty times (Greek) in the epistle." Then Dr. Hiebert quotes Norman B. Harrison: "It is the biggest word in the book." Note the frequent use of the expressions "as in him," "in whom," and "in the beloved." Every vital truth in the epistle is thus directly related to Christ.

I am writing all this so we see the importance of abiding in Jesus because all of our blessings are found only in Him. Ephesians chapter 1, verse 5 discusses our adoption as sons, verse 6 our acceptance, verse 7 our being forgiven of our sins, verses 8–10 that in our future we (the believers) will all be together with Him, verse 11 that we have an inheritance, verse 13 we were sealed with the Holy Spirit of promise, and verse 14 that the Holy Spirit is our guarantee so we have security in knowing that we will receive our inheritance, the redemption of our body. Chapter 2 speaks of our place of worship and service. I am sure you see the importance of being in Jesus by now. In Philippians chapter 3, Paul writes about the importance and the praiseworthiness of being found in Jesus.

Let me tell you why I believe what I have written here: God does not want anyone to perish (2 Peter 3:9; 1 Timothy 2:3–4), God is seeking people to worship Him (John 4:23), and Jesus prays for those who will believe the truth (John 17:20). Even in the Old Testament, God desires that men turn from their wicked ways and repent so they can live (Ezekiel 18:19–32). Paul tells Timothy to endure all things (Timothy knew the persecutions Paul had been through) for the sake of the elect, that they also may obtain the salvation which is in Christ Jesus (2 Timothy 2:10). I want to say again that God chose us in Christ when we believed in our heart the Gospel. I want you to see the importance that Jesus places on the heart; please read the Sermon on the Mount (Matthew 5:1 through 7:29).

In John chapter 15, verse 16, Jesus said to His disciples, "You did not choose me, but I chose you." So how do we interpret this? Remember from the Old Testament that God spoke with Adam, Noah, and Abraham directly, and Jacob too. There were many others to whom God spoke. On these occasions, God gave them a direct message to tell others or a certain task to perform. So here in the context of John chapter 15, we see that Jesus is talking directly to His disciples, to whom He said, "Come follow me." These are the ones who had been with Him from the beginning (John 15:27). God calls us to respond to His call to love and trust Him through the Gospel message, but with them, Jesus just said, "Come follow me." They followed because they were seeking their Messiah (John 1:35–41). Also in John 1:43–45, where Philip found Nathanael. I simply believe that Jesus knew their hearts, and that is why He chose them. Jesus even said to them He chose them and appointed them to go and bear fruit. This was said to them before they had a full understanding of who He was and why He had come. They were seeking the King of Israel, but He came to be the Savior of all mankind. They did not understand that yet here in these chapters of John, but they would later. Jesus even chose one of them so that the Scripture might be fulfilled (John 17:12, John 13:18, where Jesus quoted Psalm 41:9). So do we have an understanding of the difference between how Jesus chose them and the way He chooses us? Please notice that the condition of the heart is at the center of the way our Lord chooses.

What do we learn from reading Romans chapters 9–11? We have learned that all the covenant promises to Israel were given to men of faith, these promises had blessings from God attached to them, but they also had the responsibility of taking action to receive them, that not all of Abraham's descendants were true Israelites even though they could trace their family tree back to Abraham, but rather the true Israelite was an Israelite because of his or her faith—the children of the promise are counted as the true seed of Abraham (Galatians 3:7). Therefore, know that only those who are of faith are the sons of Abraham. Abraham also knew that God would send Jesus to take away the sins of his descendants (John 8:56, Jesus was speaking to the Jews, the Pharisees): "Abraham rejoiced to see My day, and he saw it and was glad."

Galatians 3:16: "Now to Abraham and his Seed were the promises made. He (God) does not say, 'and to seeds,' as of many, but as of one, 'and to your Seed, who is Christ.'"

In Acts 3:25, Peter is speaking and quotes Genesis 22:18 when he was telling the people about the promises made to Abraham and his descendants, "And in your seed all the families of the earth will be blessed," and Peter goes on and tells them about Jesus, who can turn them away from their iniquities. So not only did Abraham believe the promise of Isaac, but also through his descendants, Abraham believed the promise of Christ would come. Let me go on to say this: Abraham would tell his son Isaac and his grandsons about the importance of the promises and the importance of the birthright (Genesis 18:19). God says that He knew that Abraham would instruct his offspring in God's ways. So I just believe that Jacob and Esau both had heard about the ways that God had led their grandfather and their dad to the place they were living, the importance of the birthright, and the way in which both of them should conduct their lives. This is why I believe Jacob was chosen because in his heart Jacob had an interest in the birthright, which was about God's covenant promise. To me, it does not matter what we think of Jacob's intentions of wanting the birthright, but God knew Jacob's heart, and God drew Jacob to take that trip of over four hundred miles to find a wife. On the way, God revealed Himself to Jacob, and Jacob trusted in God and found his way through the circumstances of his journey. John 6:44 says, "No one can come to Me (Jesus) unless the Father who sent Me (Jesus) draws him." What happened here in Jacob's life is exactly what Romans chapter 10 is all about.

I want to summarize what Paul is teaching us here in Romans chapters 9–11. God made promises to Abraham and his descendants that can never be broken (chapter 11:29). So God chose a nation to be His witnesses, but they faltered in their quest to pursue God through His promises by trying to establish their own righteousness instead of trusting in God's. Many of the nation were not the true children of Abraham because they did not believe the Gospel message they had received through their prophets. Paul uses many verses of Scripture here in these chapters to prove his point.

Here in Romans 11:32: "For God has committed them all to disobedience, that He might have mercy on all."

Galatians 3:22: "But the Scripture has confined all under sin, that the promise by faith in Jesus Christ might be given to those who believe."

Hebrews 11:4: "For indeed the gospel was preached to us as well as to them; but the word which they heard did not profit them, not being mixed with faith in those who heard it"—or another way to say it, "since they were not united by faith with those who heeded it." In chapter 10, Paul says that his countrymen have heard the message and they knew firsthand what the message was, but many had rejected it. Because of the Jews stumbling over the chief cornerstone, and the message sent to the Gentiles being received by them and many of them believed. Does this mean that the Jews were lost forever? Paul writes "God forbid" is the answer. Paul uses himself as an example of God not casting away His people whom He foreknew. Ananias in Acts chapter 9 and Simeon and Anna in Luke chapter 2 are two more examples of God not casting away His people.

Let me submit to you, dear reader, that in these verses of chapters 9–11, the foundation of thought is that of faith. Moreover, God's plan of salvation is still ongoing because God is still working by using the mercy shown to the Gentiles as a way to make the Jewish people jealous of the mercy shown to the Gentiles that they might receive it too.

Let me conclude by saying this: our salvation is based on God knowing our hearts. He even knew our hearts before we were born (remember what God said in Isaiah 66:1–2, how He is looking on the person with a contrite spirit), so the call of God to love and trust Him comes to us on the avenue of repentance and faith. I have to ask, dear reader; are you trusting in Jesus alone for the salvation of your soul? I sure hope so!

One more thought: the fruit of the Holy Spirit that was given to us in Romans 4:23–25 when we accepted Jesus as our Savior, we became justified in God's eyes, and we received the fruit that only the Holy Spirit can give—love, joy, and peace. Then in Romans chapter 7, we see the importance of abiding in Jesus in our daily lives through reading our Bibles so we don't get overtaken by the weakness of our flesh, and we can display the fruit of the Holy Spirit back to God by being faithful in the spirit of meekness and temperance. Then in Romans chapter 12, Paul tells us how to display the fruit of the Holy Spirit by acting in longsuffering, gentleness, and goodness toward our brothers and sisters in the Lord.

Romans 12:1–2: "I beseech you therefore, brethren, by the mercies of God, that you present your bodies a living sacrifice, holy, acceptable to God, which is your reasonable service. And do not be conformed to this world, but be transformed by the renewing of your mind, that you may prove what is that good and acceptable and perfect will of God." Amen.

Respectfully,
Randall Thomas

About the Author

RANDALL THOMAS WAS born on July 4, 1947 and was raised on a dairy farm in Ohio. He was married to his wonderful wife, Juanita, after serving in the Army. He met the Lord at Faith Baptist Church in Greenville, Ohio. Then in the mid-1970s, Randy felt led to go to a good Bible school. He graduated from Tennessee Temple Bible School in the early 1980s.